paRables in action

Hidden Treasure

By Nancy I. Sanders
and Susan Titus Osborn

Illustrated by Julie Durrell

CPH.
SAINT LOUIS

D1508970

With love for my granddaughter Shelby.
May you learn more about Jesus through
reading this book. — *S.T.O.*

With love for Heather Shaner. May God's
treasure always shine from your heart.
                                    — *N.I.S.*

Parables in Action Series

Lost and Found
Hidden Treasure
Comet Campout
Moon Rocks and Dinosaur Bones

1 2 3 4 5 6 7 8 9 10   08 07 06 05 04 03 02 01 00 99

Hi! My name is Suzie. My friends and I are playing hide-and-seek at the park.

"You're it, Suzie!" shouted
Bubbles. She ran and hid behind
a tree.

The Spy hid behind the slide.

Mario and his dog, Woof, ran
behind a bush.

I closed my eyes and sat
on the swing. I counted to 100.
"… 98, 99, 100!" I yelled.
"Ready or not, here I come!"

I opened my eyes and looked
around. Where was everyone?
I peeked in the bushes. Nobody
was there. I climbed down the
hill.

Aha! I saw The Spy, but he didn't see me. He sat in the grass. He wrote notes in his spy book. I snuck up behind him. I tagged him on the back.

"Writing spy notes?" I asked. In his book I saw a map of the park.

The Spy closed his book. SLAM! He whispered in my ear. "Snork, snork, rumple."

I knew what he'd said. The Spy has been my friend for a long time. "Snork, snork, rumple" is his secret code for "no." The Spy likes to talk in secret code. Today he wasn't writing spy notes. He was drawing a spy map.

I left The Spy to find the others. I climbed the hill and saw Bubbles. She was hiding behind a tree. Today Bubbles was dressed like a cowgirl. She does TV ads. She was practicing for her next TV ad.

I snuck up on Bubbles. She saw me. Bubbles ran to the swing. I ran to the swing too. Bubbles got there first! She roped the swing with her cowgirl rope.

"I'm not it, little doggie!" she shouted. She talked like a cowgirl.

"The Spy is it," I said. "I found him first. Now I have to find Mario and Woof."

"I'll help round up the cows," Bubbles said. She pulled her rope off the swing. She carried it in her hand.

We both looked for Mario. We looked behind logs. We looked under the play fort. We even looked down the hill. All we saw was The Spy drawing his map.

Where was Mario? Once we'd gone on a field trip to a sea animal park with our class. Mario was missing at that park too!

"Maybe Mario's in trouble," Bubbles said. "Let's find him!"

"Come on!" I told The Spy. As the three of us ran, I prayed. I asked Jesus to keep Mario safe.

"WOOF! WOOF! WOOF!"
Suddenly we heard Woof barking. We ran toward the barking dog. We raced out of the park. We ran into an empty lot. There stood Mario and Woof! I said a prayer thanking Jesus for His help.

"Are you okay?" I asked.

"I'm super-duper!" Mario shouted. He pointed at the ground.

The Spy opened his spy book. He started writing notes.

Bubbles and I looked at the ground. "Did you find gold, cowboy?" Bubbles asked.

Mario shouted again. "It's better than gold. I found a dinosaur bone."

Bubbles and I looked at the ground again. Bubbles dug a little hole with her cowgirl boot.

Mario was excited. "I looked for a place to hide. Then I heard Woof barking. I ran over here. Woof dug a hole in the ground. He's always digging holes. He likes to dig for bones."

Mario pointed to a small black rock. "Look what Woof found! It's the tailbone of a Tyrannosaurus rex!"

15

The Spy wrote notes.
Bubbles and I looked at each
other. I knew what Bubbles
was thinking. "Mario's crazy as
a rattlesnake tied in a knot,"
she whispered.

I nodded. All I saw was a
rock in the hole. I turned to
Mario. "Do you really think this
is a dinosaur bone?" I asked.

"Of course!" Mario shouted.

"It looks like a rock," I said.

Mario jumped up and down.
"Of course it does. Dinosaur
bones look like rocks. But it's
not a rock. It's a bone. Isn't it,
Woof?"

Woof wagged his tail and barked. "WOOF!"

"Woof only digs for bones," Mario said. "He never digs for rocks."

"Well, cowboy," Bubbles said. "How about digging up that there gold? Take it to the sheriff. He'll tell you if it is fool's gold or not."

Mario frowned. "I can't dig it up. It's part of the dinosaur."

I frowned. "Do you think there's a whole dinosaur under there?"

Mario nodded. Woof barked again. "WOOF! WOOF! WOOF!" He ran circles around Mario.

"What is it, boy?" Mario asked.

Woof raced over to a sign. "WOOF! WOOF! WOOF!"

We followed him. The sign said, *FOR SALE: $250*.

"That's it!" Mario cried. "I'll buy the empty lot. Then the dinosaur bones will be mine."

Mario ran back to the hole. He covered the hole with dirt. Then he left. Woof followed him.

"Where are you going?" I asked.

"To buy the field!" Mario yelled.

The Spy looked at the hole. We thought about what to do.

"That cowboy may need some help," Bubbles said.

"Come on!" I shouted. The three of us ran all the way to Mario's house.

Mario sat in the front yard. Next to him was a sign. It said: *FOR SALE*. On the ground were lots of toys. It looked like a toy store.

The Spy started writing more notes. Bubbles threw her rope. She roped a toy shark.

"What are you doing?" I asked Mario.

Mario said, "I'm selling my toy collection. I need enough money to buy the empty lot."

I looked around. Mario liked to collect things. I saw his plane collection. I saw his toy fish collection. I saw his baseball card collection. He was selling everything!

A lady walked up. "A toy sale?" she asked. "It's my granddaughter's birthday." She bought lots of toys.

Within minutes, the place was crowded. Moms, dads, and kids bought Mario's toys.

I asked Jesus to help Mario not make a big mistake. I didn't think there was a dinosaur in the field. But Mario was selling EVERYTHING.

Before we knew it, Mario's yard was empty. Mario counted his money. Bubbles and I helped with the quarters and dimes. The Spy wrote down all the numbers in his book.

Mario peeked in The Spy's book. "We did it!" Mario shouted. "Two hundred and fifty dollars!"

Mario dumped the money in a bag. He ran down the street. Woof ran after him.

"Where are you going?" I shouted.

"To buy the empty lot! Meet me there in an hour!" Mario called back.

Bubbles, The Spy, and I walked
back to the lot. S-l-o-w-l-y. We had
a whole hour.

When we reached the lot, we saw Mr. Zinger.

"Hi, Nan and Larry," Mr. Zinger said. "Hi, Susan." Nan is Bubbles' real name. Larry is The Spy's name. Mr. Zinger always calls us by our real names. He is our teacher.

"What are you doing out here with the cows?" Bubbles asked.

"Mario called me. He told me to meet him at the empty lot," Mr. Zinger said.

Just then a backhoe drove up. A tall crane followed. A dump truck too. "Is Mario here?" one of the drivers asked.

I shook my head. A van drove up. On the side it said "TV NEWS." The news reporter asked, "Is Mario here?"

Just then Mario ran up. He held a paper in his hand. "Hold this," he told The Spy. "It says the field is mine."

Mario waved his hands. He pointed and shouted. He jumped up and down. The backhoe started digging. ROAR! The backhoe dumped dirt into the dump truck. THUMP! DUMP!

The hole grew bigger and bigger. More TV news vans drove up. A helicopter flew over us. More and more people came.

The hole grew even bigger!

Suddenly Mario counted to five and shouted, "PULL!" The crane pulled. Out popped the biggest bunch of bones I'd ever seen. It was a Tyrannosaurus rex!

Everyone clapped and cheered! Bubbles roped the Tyrannosaurus rex with her rope. She pretended to pull. Everyone laughed.

36

I said a prayer. I thanked Jesus
for helping Mario do the right thing.

A camera took a picture of Mario.

Mario grinned. He stood next to
the dinosaur.

Woof wagged his tail. "WOOF!"

A lady walked up to Mario. She shook his hand. "I'm from the museum. You said you'd found dinosaur bones?"

Mario grinned. "I sure did! It's the biggest treasure I've ever seen."

Bubbles and I gave Mario a high five.

Bubbles asked, "What are you going to do with all your gold, cowboy? Sell it and get rich?"

Mario patted Woof's head.

"No," he said. "I'm giving the dinosaur to the museum. I want kids everywhere to share the special treasure I found."

Woof started to dig a new hole. "WOOF!"

41

"Look," Mario cried, pointing to the hole.

"It's the toe bone of a bronto-saurus! We found another dinosaur!"

Everyone ran over to see. We all cheered!

Woof started barking. "WOOF! WOOF! WOOF!"

Parable of the Hidden Treasure

Based on Matthew 13:44

One day, Jesus told a parable:

God's kingdom is like a treasure hidden in a field.

When a man found it, he was excited. He hid it again. Then he sold all he had.

With the money, the man bought the field. He got the treasure too!

45

Mario was like that man.

He found a treasure of dinosaur bones. He was excited.

Then he sold all his toys to buy the field. He got the treasure too!

Jesus has a treasure waiting for us in heaven. This treasure is more valuable than anything else in the world!

Hi! Jesus has a treasure waiting for us in heaven. Here's one way you can put Jesus' Parable of the Hidden Treasure into ACTION!

Parables In Action

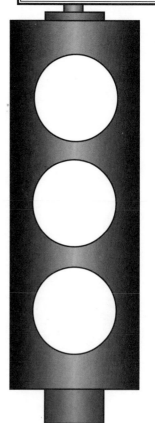

Get Ready. Talk about heaven with your friends and family. Ask them what they think heaven will look like.

Get Set. Use a black marker on white paper to make at least five pictures about heaven. Draw angels, God's throne, the Holy City, and more!

Go! Photocopy your pictures and staple them together to make coloring books. Give these coloring books to your friends and tell them about the treasure of heaven.

Suzie

Bubbles

Mario

Larry, The Spy

Mr. Zinger

Woof

Put a Parable into Action Today!

Read this story about Suzie and her friends Bubbles, Mario, and The Spy. When they play hide-and-seek in the park, one of the friends makes a surprising discovery. What will happen next?

Jesus told stories too. Stories helped His listeners understand important teachings about God. *Hidden Treasure* tells about a treasure, just like the hidden treasure in Jesus' parable. Read the parable at the end of this book. How is it like *Hidden Treasure?* How is it different?

One thing is definitely the same: God wants everyone to know that the kingdom of heaven is of great value, bought through the saving work of Jesus.

CPH®
Concordia Publishing House

Children's R
Reading Level: Grade
Interest Level: Ages 4–7
56-2036
0-570-07013-9

P8-BCB-133